In the Middle Distance

In the Middle Distance

POEMS

Linda Gregg

Graywolf Press
SAINT PAUL, MINNESOTA

Publication of this volume is made possible in part by a grant provided by the Minnesota
State Arts Board, through an appropriation by the Minnesota State Legislature; a grant
from the Wells Fargo Foundation Minnesota; and a grant from the National Endowment
for the Arts, which believes that a great nation deserves great art. Significant support
has also been provided by the Bush Foundation; Target, with support from the Target
Foundation; the McKnight Foundation; and other generous contributions from founda-
tions, corporations, and individuals. To these organizations and individuals we offer our
heartfelt thanks.

NATIONAL
ENDOWMENT
FOR THE ARTS

MINNESOTA
STATE ARTS BOARD

Published by Graywolf Press
2402 University Avenue, Suite 203
Saint Paul, Minnesota 55114
All rights reserved.

www.graywolfpress.org

Published in the United States of America

ISBN 1-55597-439-2

2 4 6 8 9 7 5 3 1
First Graywolf Printing, 2006

Library of Congress Control Number: 2005932355

Cover design: Christa Schoenbrodt, Studio Haus

Cover art: Lucas Cranach the Elder, *Venus and Cupid,* ca. 1525–27, The Metropolitan
Museum of Art, The Jack and Belle Linsky Collection, 1982 (1982.60.48) Photograph ©
The Metropolitan Museum of Art

Contents

The Lightning | 3

Even If the Gods Look Down | 4

Purity | 5

Staying After | 6

Elegance | 7

The Intercontinental Hotel | 8

The Secret Life of New York | 9

Getting Value | 11

Marfa | 12

Plenty | 13

As Is | 15

Enter with Caution | 16

The Other Excitement | 17

The Otherness | 18

Changed or Cheapened | 19

Trying to Ripen | 20

Mother My Mother | 21

The Problem of Sentences | 23

Being | 24

Beauty | 25

Waiting | 26

The Presence in Absence | 27

Turn, Turn | 28

Guilty | 29

Having It Both Ways | 30

Fragments | 31

After the Fires | 32

Silence and Glare | 33

According to the Hour | 34

"They Cripple with Beauty and Butcher with Love" | 35

Searching for the Poem | 36

The Stories Are Strenuous | 39

Bamboo and a Bird | 40

Always Alone | 41

The Test Is Whether Anything Breaks Off
    When You Roll It Down Stairs | 43

Arriving Again and Again without Noticing | 44

Quietly | 45

Not Knowing the Rules | 46

I Do Not Need the Gods to Return | 47

Searching | 48

Nine Years Later | 49

Turning into Things | 50

Now I Understand | 51

The Singers Change, the Music Goes On | 52

It Goes Away | 53

The Light Continues | 54

The Alternative | 55

Real Romance | 56

Surviving Love | 57

Backroads | 58

What's Left | 59

It Is Our Shape I Am Speaking Of | 60

Clear Sky Goes Up Farther than What Can Be Seen | 61

Parian Marble | 62

Closest It Can Get to the Human | 63

Watching the Last Boat | 64

Whoever | 65

Highway 90 | 66

FOR JACK GILBERT

Living alone with the magnitude.
So close to the laws of its nature.

In the Middle Distance

THE LIGHTNING

The bell ringing has been a great pleasure
for her during these months. But she
has been confused by the many secrets.
The fragments of stories between
upstairs and down. Like when the woman
dressed in such a beautiful white gown
with only one shoe. And that one with
no heel. And the other woman upstairs
and down. Fragments of stories.
She admitted it was her fault because
of her questions. Dreaming her own story
wanting to be part of it. And never explained.
The strange life she would take upstairs
and the waiting. The lightning in the night
over Iowa cornfields. Talking about love
and its dangers. About what happens when
you lay the new image over the old.

EVEN IF THE GODS LOOK DOWN

Hawks are flying slowly high above
the barren ground where love
used to be. The heavy salmon
are dying as they struggle with the last
of their strength in the shallows
to get home. Even if there were gods
what could they do about love?
The heart is sometimes tender
but still is slayed.
Just as a deer is killed.
Killed and eaten. The liver
first with onion while the beast
is hung outside to bleed.

PURITY

I'm walking on farm road 2810 again,
alone as always. Unless you want to count
the Border Patrol. Or the police cars
that go by with their strange maneuvers
in front of me and pull off into
the mowed grass on the side. Then turn
and come back. Stalling and facing me.
Waiting until a car approaches
from far away. It passes and the police
follow it toward town. Leaving me
with animals, insects and birds.
And the silence. I walk toward the sun
which is always going down.

STAYING AFTER

I grew up with horses and poems
when that was the time for that.
Then Ginsberg and Orlovsky
in the Fillmore West when
everybody was dancing. I sat
in the balcony with my legs
pushed through the railing,
watching Janis Joplin sing.
Women have houses now, and children.
I live alone in a kind of luxury.
I wake when I feel like it,
read what Rilke wrote to Tsvetaeva.
At night I watch the apartments
whose windows are still lit
after midnight. I fell in love.
I believed people. And even now
I love the yellow light shining
down on the dirty brick wall.

Elegance

All that is uncared for.
Left alone in the stillness
in that pure silence married
to the stillness of nature.
A door off its hinges,
shade and shadows in an empty room.
Leaks for light. Raw where
the tin roof rusted through.
The rustle of weeds in their
different kinds of air in the mornings,
year after year.
A pecan tree, and the house
made out of mud bricks. Accurate
and unexpected beauty, rattling
and singing. If not to the sun,
then to nothing and to no one.

The Intercontinental Hotel

Walking into the elegant bar at last
call. Really just to sit down after
walking for an hour in the summer night.
There is a faint singing, out of reach
in the emptiness. Reminding me of long ago.
Did I catch the ball when it was thrown?
Have the soul and its ghost given up
and gone back to sleep? Is the heart
supposed to be passive and just wait?
Or should it start talking, even to itself?
Like the grand bouquet on this table
that no one's looking at. Tempting me
to sing back. Singing to myself
as I leave. Leaving so much with me.

The Secret Life of New York

She decided to walk there.
Put the high heels in a backpack.
Walked down two flights, through
two doors and up three steps to the street.
When she reached the National Wholesale
Liquidators, a black man
gave her a torn card numbered 110
and took the backpack.
She chose some biscuits that cost
twenty-nine cents and a box
of foaming bath granules
for a dollar sixty-seven. Went upstairs
to see if there were any bras
without underwires. Found one.
It was not as plain as she wanted
but she tried it on over her undershirt.
It was too big. Paid for the two items
and started walking. Four Asian women
raced by to see an Asian man
in a silver convertible. One turned back,
saying he was not as good looking
as she expected. On the other side
of Houston, two old women stood
next to card tables, each with
two cans of kidneys beans. One had
a few boxes of macaroni and cheese

on sale. At the bookstore
she sat outside and changed
into a good jacket and the heels.
Then went into the party
at the back of the store.

Getting Value

My elderly friend of many years arrived
last winter at my door with his nose
dripping onto the floor, and shaking
so hard you could hear his teeth clatter.
It was hard to get his clothes off
and him onto the sofa bed in my living room.
Filling me with memories of what
he used to be. What the French call
"monsters." (Like Rodin.) His poetry is
deeper now. Bigger, and more tender
than ever. We wonder about the newness
of the old. And how much is missing.
He forgets names and directions.
Surely there is a hollowing out,
but how much that is left is more than
the past was? The Shakespeare who stopped
writing. And the crippled Leonardo.
What about our very old god who is
now making his problematical children?

MARFA

They said they were going to telephone me
here in faraway Marfa, Texas, to ask me about
my poetry, past and future. I am here struggling
with the desert and used-up words.
Stillness, sacred, death, peace and farness.
With God's body, dreamless and sleeping
while awake. Nothing between me and it.
Empty and willing to be judged by Heaven.
Readiness to be received. God might be the old
version who struck people down because somebody
asked him to. A kind of courtyard for the Mafia.
The desert after rain with a three-colored rainbow.
A place of your-guess-is-as-good-as-mine.
Christ as the sun going down when the border
patrol cars are dragging tires on the dirt road
every evening to look for footprints
the next morning. I keep thinking that if I go
alone into the size of this silence, we can
straighten things out. To know what to question,
and what to believe. How to let my heart
split open. To print in clear light
the changing register of this grand world.

PLENTY

I called my sister the day before
she had to leave Marfa to drive
across the desert in an old truck
on Highway 10, in the blinding
late June heat. I said
I was trying to write a pastoral
poem while reading Virgil.
Asked if she remembered the names
of the flowers our mother planted
around the house. Louise said,
"Daffodils! (The old-fashioned kind
Mom got from the Dickson ranch.
Ruffle-edged.) Daphne, narcissus,
hyacinth, Chinese wisteria, roses,
lilac, mock-orange, clover and violets."
"And quince," I said. "And the sweet
peas growing just before the woods.
And myrtle." Louise said she didn't
like myrtle or oleander. She said
she liked the flags-in-the-moss.
"What about the flowers in the woods?"
I said. "What about trillium, hound's
tongue and spring maidens?" "Mom,"
she said, "used to point them out
when they started to bloom."

"Tiger bells," I said. "Purple iris
in the fields, white iris in the woods."
"Indian paintbrush," Louise said.
"And most of all," I said, "coral root."

As Is

Pay attention, talk to no one unless
you are buying food or borrowing a book.
Or asking for directions to the border,
or the canyon, or the river with a pool.
Always formal. Poor with poor.
It's not the same here. No Greek ruins.
No fragment with legs of walking horses
painted delicately on it. No part
of a lion on bits of a glazed vase.
Like a code to tell of the world they knew
would be destroyed. Here there is no need.
The rabbit's groin is ripped open
on the road. When you find a bird's wing
there is a flattened small bird attached.
A ranch at evening, the sun leaving,
antelope standing and the other birds
flying. All of it meaning the same thing.

ENTER WITH CAUTION

There will be the smell of Greek sunlight with her
when she walks from the train to the tram that goes
to Monastiraki Square. She will walk to the brothel-
turned-hotel from there. The next day there will be
the smell of crude oil on the freighter from Piraeus
to an island. She will be watching almond trees on
the mountain for most of the next seven years after that.
A goat bleating near its mother by the stone house.
The well-cover bangs shut in October.
The sea is too strong all winter, roaring
even when it's silent. Covering her head completely
when she walks to town along the edge of the shore.
The shepherd-boy sitting on a table at the back
of the taverna, surrounded by happy farmers giving him
wine to drink. Buying fresh donuts from the man carrying
them through the village on his head every Monday.
Swimming in the sea all afternoon, then eating
the melon. Twelve-year-old Stephanie in only the bottom
of her bathing suit, standing with great bunches of grapes,
laughing and jumping up and down in the aqua water.
Walking to the mountain where gods have been honored,
the brightness of the sun stunning. Seeing broken
libation cups in the weeds. Living alone with
the magnitude. So close to the laws of its nature.

The Other Excitement

If I go back into memory it's not
because I like it, but because
that's where the hard things are.
Nothing that gets excited. Almost
ripe and the beauty of things
in the middle distance.
Going down the mountain.

The Otherness

Of course there is the otherness,
right away inside you when
the doe steps carefully down
the embankment. Then clatter
of hoof and the dappled water
with leaf shade. The otherness
and the invisible until you came.

CHANGED OR CHEAPENED

The memory of things I have loved
seems worn, built over, changed or cheapened.
But other times are still wildly fresh.
Some of the problem is because I don't
live there now. The mountain might be out
of place, or the ocean might get mixed
with the desert. I don't mind if things
are reduced to a simplicity.
But it is important that the reduction
does not go too far. The essence
has to be protected. Otherwise
my life will be like those wooden
German toys. Each piece rudimentary
and general: a dog, a tree, some sheep.
There must always be the bite of
the creek's smell. The face of the man
I love when he was asleep. I worry
that talking about it will turn
these sentences into words
instead of the experience. I want to keep
the real world that is inside me,
and its stillness.

Trying to Ripen

I thought if I lived alone
in stillness, God would be closer.
Or if I lived beyond aging and dying.
Now I look at the birds
and the orchard with longing.
There is ripe fruit on the ground.
It is time for migration,
but I am still not transformed.
I have become like the desert.
Today I saw a large red snake
and a covey of quail
strong enough now to fly over
the fence. I saw distance.

MOTHER MY MOTHER

if my mother was a
tiger it wouldn't matter
if my mother was mud
if mud was money
then it wouldn't matter
if mother would promise
to stay away from the mountain
my mountain
if it could be kept so
guards stand guard but no
world would fail
mother mother mother
money money money
freedom in ruins money spent
power ruining power
the fern hurt
if my mother was a hippopotamus
then she could wallow
to her heart's content
walk up through the green hills
the war rages
and the roar of the creek
in January although it blocks
out the sound does not stop
or heal what continues to kill
the young and strong and wounded

if I could get enough
away from people
where there was much more sky
than land
if I could get closer to the light
where there is more light
where most of it is light

THE PROBLEM OF SENTENCES

A sentence is an idea. An idea with urgency.
A feeling for the sun before it rises.
The imagination loves the wall of a building,
loves the floor and the square window
that looks out on it. The scent of jasmine
is how the plant climbs up the wall
built by the Knights of Rhodes.
But the sentence stresses the meaning,
making us notice an unruly jasmine against
the orderly stone wall. We say our bus
went down through the village of the insane,
or that the eucalyptus trees were tall.
That we saw a man dragging a big branch.
The sun will return whether you smile or cry,
clap or burn candles. But when I say *whether,*
the sentence may be thinking, *even so.*

BEING

The woman walks up the mountain
and then down. She wades into the sea
and out. Walks to the well,
pulls up a bucket of water
and goes back into the house.
She hangs wet clothes.
Takes clothes back to fold them.
Every evening she crochets
from six until dark.
Birds, flowers, stars. Her rabbit lives
in an empty donkey pen. The sea is out
there as far as the stars.
Always quiet.
No one there. She may not believe
in anything. Not know
what she is doing. Every morning
she waters the geranium plant.
And the leaves smell like lemons.

Beauty

There she was on *Entertainment Tonight.*
Someone had caught a glimpse of Bardot
after all these years. Brigitte Bardot
running through the trees, across a meadow,
a dog running with her. The hair still long.
Then another part showing her on the patio,
aged. (Sun-damaged, we say.) The violation
of beauty never happens just once.
When my father heard his beloved dog
had chased and killed the rancher's sheep,
he went right out and shot it. Because,
he said, once they ran with the pack
and tasted blood, it would never stop.

WAITING

When I chewed a bay leaf and rubbed
sage on my hands and arms, I believed
it was in order not to scare the deer.
Which was true. Later I thought it was
so my soul could be read by God.
Now I suspect it is a way for me
to become hidden. When you came to court me
for my body and hair, I was not there,
even though I was washed and dressed
for the occasion. Did you see me stare
beneath the courtesies? I was waiting
for someone to want that. To want
the moon by itself. For the quiet
of the herd. Of the stones under the water
in the creek flickering. Seeming to move,
but not moving. Together with everything
that's here.

The Presence in Absence

Poetry is not made of words.
I can say it's January when
it's August. I can say, "The scent
of wisteria on the second floor
of my grandmother's house
with the door open onto the porch
in Petaluma," while I'm living
an hour's drive from the Mexican
border town of Ojinaga.
It is possible to be with someone
who is gone. Like the silence which
continues here in the desert while
the night train passes through Marfa
louder and louder, like the dogs whining
and barking after the train is gone.

Turn, Turn

She walks around in her poems
like circling a statue. Noticing
how it is changed by light and modified
according to her gait. Seeing how
a chunk of marble becomes a god
if a mantle is put on it. The way
Autolycus changes everything by
singing about the "white sheet
bleaching on the hedge." Or the ancient
Chinese ladies carrying perfumed fans
to speak through. In this world where
we keel over because of the surprising
singing in us, and the quiet of the soul.

GUILTY

Who, seeing the wounded one,
does not wonder about the cause,
wonder if she is to blame?
Was the antelope already limping
or was the woman in love?
What if it was a crime of passion?
If he wounded her that was in love
who but God would know? She plants
seeds now that will grow
into flowers. Sings every song
known in the heart by heart.

Having It Both Ways

I was abandoning the heart for lack
of evidence. The poems I wrote
this summer were far from impressive.
Then the voice said, "For God's sake,
the Mediterranean sunlight is pouring
out each morning through
the balcony door onto white marble."
It's the difference between what I have lived
and the thing made. Love depends on something
happening. The monuments to eternity
can be found, picked up, sat upon while the
day dies. Giving in after giving in.

FRAGMENTS

You can't call the exhausted people on
the 1 or 9 line beautiful. Especially
the drunk at the back yelling and stumbling
and grabbing the pole gracefully just
in time. Beauty has a strangeness.
The old man leaning against the cement
column at the station on 42nd (when I
changed to the N or R) has three holes
in his pants. Neon and magazine covers
about a new couple. I believe everyone
is going home. This is the way.

After the Fires

Now that you are old, you have moved inland,
surrounded by trees and a river hidden below.
You walk there with your life inside you.
The scenes, the arrangements and dissertations
on the bounty of women, the flecks of their color,
and all the rest. With your age upon you,
your boxes of papers and pictures cut out of
the *National Geographic* ranging from the forties
to the present, to know the world that was yours.
It makes me remember the fires that were built
on the beaches when I was young. Huge fires
made out of what was there. I remember what
they looked like when the fires went out.
Plenty of logs left blackened, held by the wet
and high tides. I stand with the size
of the burnt-out fires the morning after
and listen to the quiet young ocean.

Silence and Glare

I get out of the car. Stand still
and listen. Look at the abandoned house,
generally. Has the plaster fallen off?
If so, how long have the adobe bricks
been exposed to rain? A house
made of mud and straw otherwise can last
for centuries. I walk to the door
with an uncovered window. Watch a crowd
of bees crawling up the other side
of the glass. Look through windows
not covered. Try to see
if there is a floor or only dirt.
I walk around the house on dry earth
and weeds so hard they push
up through my rubber soles.
A place to be now that love is gone.

According to the Hour

Years later, back on the island
in absolute light, I am trying
to remember what it was like.
There was seeing, then passion,
and then ravishment. After that
the punishment. It is important to me
that the world has not changed.
This morning the woman across the road
came out and pulled up an armload
of onions and went away.
The mountain of the gods is far
from town. The sea changes
its color according to the hour,
becoming palest just before dark.

"They Cripple with Beauty and Butcher with Love"

Eight years later the woman is given
a house for five months at the edge of town
in the desert. It's August and the desert is green.
When rain falls, she drives beyond the dark clouds.
Past an antelope, legs resting under it,
head raised, white marks. Drives slowly around
a turtle. If the man lied about love,
or even if it was true, there was immense damage.
When she woke, she was at the beginning where
love ends. Beauty everywhere on the road.
Silence inside her body in the clear
evening air, near the Mexican border.

Searching for the Poem

I.

The boat of the bible was
pushed into the reeds. Our chanting
is the stolen property of the sea.
Bathing is our clothing, is the mountain
I see in you. I walk up in the heat
to remember its weight. Which has
something to do with it. We are struck
dumb by what we call truth.
Having to match the foreignness of stone.
Our speech is far from the click
and shift of broken glass, making
the new colored pictures we try
to memorize in our sleep.
We are strengthened even by defeat,
honoring most what is strangest among us.

II.

I'm standing with a tree while
the sun rises, proud of the night.
She pushed the infant into the reeds
to keep the secret. Using language
for imitation. To keep the mountain
of the beloved. I walk up the mountain
in the heat to know belief. The glass
image shifts and clicks in our sleep.
Changes into another mystery
to turn the pages.

III.

The thing we are trying to say
is in the language of leaves.
We take our chanting from the sea
and clothe ourselves in the instruments
of water. We can never speak
its language. In the book they made
a boat of our reeds to hide
the child. We go down and forth,
proud to live with the night.
We walk up the mountain to relearn
the weight. To keep inside the beloved.
When we sleep the universe shifts
and clicks. We memorize each
new image and hide it for safety.
For our chanting. Get as close as possible
without knowing. Draw it with a stick.

The Stories Are Strenuous

The story was about Orpheus getting
his head cut off by women
who had gathered under a tree.
How his head continued to sing.
When do we get to say that it's not true?
I saw him yesterday evening
walking through the village,
offending the neighborhood,
alarming the authorities. Breaking
the laws wholeheartedly
by the sweetness of his singing.

Bamboo and a Bird

In the subway late at night.
Waiting for the downtown train
at Forty-second Street.
Walking back and forth
on the platform.
Too tired to give money.
Staring at the magazine covers
in the kiosk. Someone passes me
from behind, wearing an orange vest
and dragging a black hose.
A car stops and the doors open.
All the faces are plain.
It makes me happy to be
among these people
who leave empty seats
between each other.

Always Alone

There was a place. It was not important.
A narrow street next to the sea in the town
where I waited for the bus to take me
back up to my house on top of the mountain.
I would buy a bottle of water and sit
on the step across from the wharf,
in the shade if I was lucky. I watched
the beaten-up fishing boats tied to the pier.
The fishermen sold their catch alongside.
Or sat idle on the decks, sometimes cooking
on small grills. Mostly I looked away,
to another mountain where I felt
the goddess used to be. Where I walked
so often in her absence. Finding
ancient shards, negotiating for my soul
with the leftover facts of the Earth.
Reconciling with what love is. Always alone.
Usually it was evening and I would be tired.
I would watch the boats, hear the Aegean,
consider the mountain that I had been intimate with.
Sometimes I would take a fragment
from my bag and spit on it. Or splash
on the last of my drinking water to see
if anything was there. Maybe a piece

of the classical black glaze
or the shadow of a flower. Maybe even
part of a maiden. In the pleasure
of the whole thing. Still a secret.

The Test Is Whether Anything Breaks Off When You Roll It Down Stairs

A dress hangs on the far wall
of a doorless room. Hot dry air,
hot dry light. The house has only
framing boards for a roof. A bathtub
sits alone outside. The stillness
eating the absence. A stuffed couch
and train tracks beyond. What's gone
makes what's left silent. The clatter,
roar and screams of the train
disappear into the hush.

Arriving Again and Again
without Noticing

I remember all the different kinds of years.
Angry, or brokenhearted, or afraid.
I remember feeling like that
walking up the mountain along the dirt path
to my broken house on the island.
And long years of waiting in Massachusetts.
The winter walking and hot summer walking.
I finally fell in love with all of it:
dirt, night, rock and far views.
It's strange that my heart is as full
now as my desire was then.

QUIETLY

Now there is neither Hart Crane's "The dice of drowned
men's bones," or Blake's orchestra of angels.
Here bells are ringing, roosters crowing
and the doves' wings flapping. All sounds
are of faith in the graveyard behind this church
that slopes steeply down toward the far sea.
Some coffins have photographs on them.
Some with housed candles. Dry earth
and pine trees. The way David Park
would paint a few figures standing in the sea.
Quiet. In the moment. Outside the self
but near. Not knowing them. Painting them
simply. Red mark for a mouth, or blue
for the sea. Like the woman in the graveyard,
alone, turning left toward her dead son.
Replacing the old flowers with the new.
Late in June, nearly nine o'clock in the evening
where it is still light.

Not Knowing the Rules

The two white-bellied antelope stood still
as I approached on the farm road at evening,
and three birds flew away. The air was clear
the way it is on the desert after rain,
the sky bright. I was wondering why,
besides the beauty, I was there. And how close
I felt to death. Waiting for the heart
to revive. Between objects and desire.
I waded on through the brilliant light
that comes here just before dark. Shining
on the grass in front of me from the back.

I Do Not Need the Gods to Return

I do not need the gods to return. I have
seen the fragments. Have weighed them
in my hand, one at a time in the heat.
One at a time, in the dry dirt. Oregano,
sage and thyme. I don't need Orpheus
to sing. I walk down the esplanade at night.
I pass one loud bar after the other.
On the left the sea, bigger and stronger
after dark. Orpheus put down his lyre
centuries ago. Who knows what the women
believe now that they are not guarded.
Who can tell if it is easier now. The wide fig
trees shade me either way. It has been
suggested that we should go back to the source.
The rain and fire that gave birth to all
of it. The paintings on jars. Burnt things.
And Aphrodite so much like a queen.
The cracking of almonds, the plowing
of the fields. The broken libation cup unbroken.
I don't need the old gods to be believed.
No Orpheus to sing again.

SEARCHING

Yesterday they threw green branches
on the narrow stone street between
the houses. Women sat neatly outside
the chapel in a row of chairs,
waiting for their turn to go in
when somebody came out. I am not
Greek or a bird, so I waited for
the off hours to stand in front
of the old icons. To look
into their solemn eyes.
Each one slightly different, like people.

Nine Years Later

What cannot be netted,
trapped or eaten.
This early sunlight
is cold, and the windows
are closed against it.
The pleasure in seeing
memory through the failure
of it. Of a place with a house
in it. Of him watching
as she walked straight through
the field of dry, standing weeds
to enter the sea. That now
was before this now.
That woman without
before this without.

Turning into Things

"I sleep with thee, and wake with thee, /
And yet thou are not there," wrote Clare
from the Northampton Asylum in 1842,
nine years after his wife's death.
It fills me with tenderness,
the way the sun blots out everything
when it's too powerful. I think of
turning into the things around him.
A table, a chair. A windowsill.
Hieroglyphics that will take years
to read. To make the day rise
out of the heart's darkness.

Now I Understand

Something was pouring out. Filling the field
and making it vacant. A wind blowing them
sideways as they moved forward. The crying
as before. Suddenly I understood why they left
the empty bowls on the table, in the empty hut
overlooking the sea. And knew the meaning
of the heron breaking branches, spreading
his wings in order to rise up out of the dark
woods into the night sky. I understood about
the lovers and the river in January.
Heard the crying out as a battlement,
of greatness, and then the dying began.
The height of passion. Saw the breaking
of the moon and the shattering of the sun.
Believed in the miracle because of the half heard
and the other half seen. How they ranged
and how they fed. Let loose their cries.
One could call it the agony in the garden,
or the paradise, depending on whether
the joy was at the beginning, or after.

The Singers Change, the Music Goes On

No one really dies in the myths.
No world is lost in the stories.
Everything is lost in the retelling,
in being wondered at. We grow up
and grow old in our land of grass
and blood moons, birth and goneness.
We live our myth in the recurrence,
pretending we will return another day.
Like the morning coming every morning.
The truth is we come back as a choir.
Otherwise Eurydice would be forever
in the dark. Our singing brings her
back. Our dying keeps her alive.

It Goes Away

I give everything away and it goes away,
into the dusty air,
onto the face of the water
that goes away beyond our seeing.
I give everything away
that has been given to me:
the voices of children under clouds,
the men in the parks at the chess tables,
the women entering and leaving bakeries.
God who came here by rock, by tree, by bird.
All things silent in my seeing.
All things believable in their leaving.
Everything I have I give away
and it goes away.

The Light Continues

Every evening, an hour before
the sun goes down, I walk toward
its light, wanting to be altered.
Always in quiet, the air still.
Walking up the straight empty road
and then back. When the sun
is gone, the light continues
high up in the sky for a while.
When I return, the moon is there.
Like a changing of the guard.
I don't expect the light
to save me, but I do believe
in the ritual. I believe
I am being born a second time
in this very plain way.

The Alternative

Maybe this is an imitated life. Morning light
on treetops, a pigeon flying to where the sun
is coming from. An iron fire escape on a dappled
wall opposite. Dead leaves that have not yet fallen
and perhaps won't until spring's new growth
forces them. Or the desert time and the emptiness
mirrored in me. The silence and my so-called soul.
It is cause for alarm when the singer is driven
from the song. I like to think this quiet in me
is prayerful, but I suspect these words are
a nervous typewriter rattling between God and man.
The heart's calling out for Him to listen.
To do something. But we continue the cover-up,
lying ourselves into belief. The whole list of it
running down the page: yogurt, beer, corn oil,
paper towels, love and the mystery.

Real Romance

Romance needs a blankness
to its depth. And energy to give
it size. I have gone back
to myths and found them empty.
I have chosen goat bells instead.
Church bells, flowers blooming
above the walls. Evidence
of fig trees in the underworld's
light and centuries of purity.

Surviving Love

I work hard at managing, grateful
and spare. I try to forgive all trespasses
and give thanks for the desert. Rejoice
in being alive here in my simple world.
Each evening I walk for an hour, paying
attention to real things. The plover
sweeping at my face to get me away from
its ground nest. An ant carrying the wing
of a butterfly like a flag in the wind.
A grasshopper eating a dead grasshopper.
The antelope close up, just staring at me.
Back in the house, I lie down in the heat
for a nap, realizing forgiveness is hard
for the wounded. Near the border,
between this country and the next one.

Backroads

She might be doing it to protect herself.
Maybe to hold onto what love
there is left. She might have come
to where she thinks the singing is,
in the dying Texas grasses.
Where the hawk refuses to leave
the long, shiny black snake that it grips
with both claws, head erect, beak pointing
to its own breast, waiting for her to leave.

What's Left

Could the soul be like a bulb under
the ground? Not just mine, but anyone's.
Any time. Poems written one
at a time, by one man at a time.
Maybe by a father who chose to leave
the city. To leave a good agency
for a rough house in the country with
a tree. Lots of trees. And a view.
And the world turning around and around
until early spring. The details
could be sandals (new sandals)
or his kids peeing in the grass
behind the house. The sun
coming up and the kids running out
from behind the house asking if
the blunt tip of the top of the leaf
was the one they planted last year.
And is its name narcissus or daffodil.

It Is Our Shape I Am Speaking Of

It is the weight more than the night.
The universe with its speed limits.
With its sound barriers, its shape
more than the stars. My body more
than the talking. We don't know
for certain, but we think it is
the shape of an animal.
I imagine I am carrying a box
with darkness in it. I believe
it contains the other. It has
the weight.

CLEAR SKY GOES UP FARTHER
THAN WHAT CAN BE SEEN

The soul could be a stone,
the writhing of a snake
wrapping its body around a hawk.
Talons embedded in the open jaw
are without feeling, but have
everything to do with life.
Sky does not speak. Night knows
nothing of sight. Rain does not
know it grows the grain.
Stone does not know it wears out.

Parian Marble

I was walking in the fields with a friend
and asked what the farmers do when they plow up
something extraordinary. He said it depends
on what it's worth. They take it to a middleman.
"Look at that," I said, and picked up a five-pound
marble head of Eros. The cheeks protected
the smile but otherwise it was beaten up.
A crack down the forehead and under one eye
made it seem to be frowning. Behind us were
four bushes: sage, thyme, oregano, and mirtia.
The sun was going down. I would like to hold
something up against ruin. To show how the heart
and spirit pass the test. The look on the face
was understanding and blissful. The light changed
and I hid it inside a bush for another two thousand years.

Closest It Can Get to the Human

Out on the desert
all the views are farness.
Miniature mountain ranges
in all directions,
folded and put away.
A heart still beating.
Air quieter than our breath.
Walking in the pure light
as the sun goes down.
Memory washing off.
What's left is the world.
A place, a road
where you can walk the last
of each day, the sun finally
forgiving in its lesser light.
Something to walk toward.

Watching the Last Boat

The crash is inside.
In slow motion. Splinters
in the mind's confusion.
Each evening the last boat goes
across to the other island.
When it is too dark to see,
I watch anyhow, remembering
how I wept that day in the Met
over a last self-portrait
by Rembrandt. The guard telling me
again and again it was closing time.

Whoever

You are not even dead yet.
I saw you again this morning
in Penn Station. In your disguise.
Small, thin, elderly. Dressed
haphazardly in unbuttoned layers.
With the cane, cap and scarf.
Unloved, but not as invisible
as you want. I don't know what to feel.
I am glad to see you sometimes.
I think there is a tenderness
in you. Like the way a bird flies.
Other times I think it is to keep
people away. Always it is unrehearsed
need. A fist of need. Never having
food set before you.

Highway 90

An owl lands on the side
of the road. Turns its head
to look at me going fast,
window open to the night
on the desert. Clean air,
and the great stars.
I'm trying to decide
if this is what I want.

Acknowledgments

Agenda Poetry (UK): "The Lightning," "Having It Both Ways,"
   "I Do Not Need the Gods to Return"
Agni: "The Singers Change, the Music Goes On"
Green Light: "Turn, Turn"
Hayden's Ferry Review: "As Is," "Not Knowing the Rules,"
   "The Presence in Absence"
The Kenyon Review: "Guilty," "Silence and Glare," "Surviving Love"
Lyric: "Backroads," "Staying After"
Manoa: "Clear Sky Goes Up Farther than What Can Be Seen,"
   "It Goes Away"
Mid-American Review: "Nine Years Later," "Turning into Things"
The New Yorker: "Beauty," "Elegance," "Getting Value,"
   "Now I Understand," "The Otherness," "The Problem of
   Sentences," "Whoever," "The Secret Life of New York,"
   "Arriving Again and Again without Noticing"
Ontario Review: "Always Alone," "Bamboo and a Bird," "Closest It
   Can Get to the Human," "Even If the Gods Look Down,"
   "The Secret Life of New York," "The Test Is Whether Anything
   Breaks Off When You Roll It Down Stairs," "Trying to Ripen,"
   "Watching the Last Boat"
Ploughshares: "'They Cripple with Beauty and Butcher with Love'"

Thanks to the Patrick Lannan Foundation for a residency during which
parts of this book were written. And for a Lannan Literary Fellowship.

I want to thank my friends for their kindness during the five years I was
writing this book (and Timothy Liu for also typing up this manuscript).

LINDA GREGG is the author of five previous books of poetry: *Things and Flesh, Chosen by the Lion, The Sacraments of Desire, Alma,* and *Too Bright to See.* Her honors include fellowships from the Guggenheim Foundation, the Lannan Literary Foundation, and the National Endowment for the Arts. She teaches at Princeton University and lives in New York City.

In the Middle Distance has been typeset in Adobe Garamond.

Book design by Rachel Holscher.
Composition at Prism Publishing Center.
Manufactured by Sheridan Books on acid-free paper.